LOVE AND SENTIMENT

DAVID LOVEDAY

Table of Content

Introduction

The most effective method to Get a Lady to Become hopelessly enamored with You.

In the event that there's a lady you really love and care about, you might be energetic for her to respond your sentiments. While you can't make somebody go gaga for you, there are a few things you can do to work on your possibilities. By getting some margin to show a lady you're a tomfoolery, caring individual, you might have the option to win her affection.

Part 1

Figuring out Fascination

1.Become familiar with some science. You can definitely relax; there won't be a test. Notwithstanding, fascination is about science, and explicitly, a gathering of synthetic substances called "monoamines." These synthetics send messages between your cerebrum and your body, and they're the explanation love can in a real sense make your skin shiver or prompt you to fail to remember your name when you're around the lady of your fantasies.

- Dopamine (where we get "dope") is a "vibe great" synapse liable for remunerations and inspiration, in addition to other things. At the point when you're around an individual you're drawn to, dopamine is delivered into your mind, causing you to partake in the time you spend together and need a greater amount of it.

• Norepinephrine, now and again known as noradrenaline (however not equivalent to adrenaline) is liable for sending messages to your focal sensory system. It concludes what means quite a bit to zero in on out of nowhere. At the point when you forget about time and wind up enjoying 5 hours out on the town with somebody, you're into, norepinephrine has concluded that the lady you love is a higher priority than any of the other data around you.

• Serotonin directs a large group of capabilities, including state of mind, rest, internal heat level, and sexual craving. At the point when your skin begins to shiver around that unique individual, this is on the grounds that serotonin has decreased your internal heat level, making your skin somewhat more conductive of power. Really supernatural stuff.

• People may likewise transmit pheromones like different creatures do, despite the fact that researchers aren't precisely certain assuming they work the same way. You can't intentionally smell pheromones; however, your body gets on others', concluding its thought process is appealing and what isn't.

Perceive that it isn't about you. Since so a lot is down to how synthetic compounds communicate in every individual's body, don't think about it literally on the off chance that the lady you're keen on doesn't return your advantage. It most likely has nothing to do with you personally. Concentrates on show that your mind chooses what's appealing in just one moment, and it's not exactly inside your control.

• Research has even demonstrated the way that taking hormonal contraceptives can change a lady's "type" at specific focuses during the month. Natural chemistry: it's some strange stuff.

Get familiar with some way to express affection. No, this type isn't the flattery you could propose during a visit. This is tied in with distinguishing the messages that non-verbal communication emits when we're drawn to another person. There are a couple of essential messages that your non-verbal communication conveys when you are keen on somebody:

• I'm free

• I'm receptive and open

• I'm intrigued

• I'm prolific

2.Check her body situating. Envision that you've run into the lady you're keen on at the bistro. You don't know whether she is keen on you. Analyze how she's holding her body for certain hints.

• "Open" non-verbal communication incorporates loose, uncrossed arms and legs and looking vertical occasionally. "Shut" non-verbal communication incorporates crossed arms or legs, body strain, and maintaining your attention on something like your telephone.

• The heading of her feet may likewise let you know something. Assuming they're highlighted you, she is reasonable inclination into the connection.

• In the event that she's holding something between you, like a satchel or bookbag, this could be a sign she's attempting to flag distance. In the event that she gets your attention, grins, and moves the bookbag out of the seat opposite her, it's a decent wagered she's flagging "I'm free."

3.Visually engage. The eyes are the windows to the spirit. They're likewise great hints regarding regardless of whether somebody is keen on you. Eye to eye connection conveys a lot of messages, including some you probably won't know about.

• Visually connect with her, and keep up with it for 4-5 seconds. Give her a grin. In the event that she returns your look and grins back, you might be fortunate.

• Eye to eye connection while you're chatting with somebody signals interest and commitment. In the event that she's taking a gander at you around 70% of the time while you're talking and around half of the time while she's talking, a decent sign she's keen on the communication. (You can flag your advantage by following similar proportions.)

• At the point when we're stirred (through pressure, sexual longing, what have you) our students expand. Assuming that her understudies look enlarged, she might be eager to see you.

4.Streak her an energetic grin. Assuming she returns your grin, it could flag that she partakes in your cooperation. Nonetheless, certain individuals likewise grin when they're anxious or awkward. Watch which muscles move when she grins.

• Real, or Duchenne, grins, utilize the muscles around the eyes as well as around the mouth. Counterfeit grins will generally just utilize the muscles around the mouth (albeit certain individuals are truly adept at faking). In the event that she isn't grinning with her eyes, she might be feeling awkward or attempting to pacify you.

5.Look at some science. People experience specific physiological responses when they're drawn to another person. While these aren't widespread, they can assist with educating you about whether she's simply being courteous or whether she's as keen on you as you are in her.

• Flushing or becoming flushed. At the point when we're excited, blood races to our cheeks. (This is one justification for why a few ladies wear become flushed.) Individuals may likewise flush when they're apprehensive or humiliated, however, so don't depend on this as your main prompt.

• Plumper, redder lips. That blood doesn't simply hurry to our cheeks. It additionally goes to the lips, which can seem more full and redder as they load up with blood. (Subsequently, why a few ladies wear lipstick.) Licking the lips is likewise a decent sign that the other individual is drawn to you.

6.Draw a little nearer. Try not to attack anybody's very own space, yet if, say, she's gone up for some espresso half and half you could get up and get a few napkins.

This will allow you the opportunity to give her a whiff of your pheromones (recollect those synthetic compounds that signal the other individual's mind, saying "Hello! I'm hot!").

• On the off chance that you're now cooperating with the lady of your fantasies, incline in somewhat closer or slant your head. Besides the fact that these sign that you're keen on the cooperation, they can likewise send those substance love-couriers traveling her direction.

7.Bet with an initial ploy. These are otherwise called "pickup lines," or here and there "conversation starters." Be that as it may, you don't need to be dreadful or presumptuous to successfully utilize an initial ruse. Researchers recommend that there are three kinds of openers, and they fluctuate in their adequacy:

• Direct: These tell the truth, straightforward, get focused openers. For instance, "Howdy, you're really adorable. Could I at any point get you a beverage?" or "I'm somewhat modest, however I'd very much want to get to know you." as a general rule, men will more often than not favor getting these from likely significant others.

• Harmless: These beginning a discussion, however don't go straightforwardly in for the objective. For instance, "What espresso would you suggest?" or "There's an unfilled seat at my table, might you want to stay here?" as a general rule, ladies will more often than not favor getting these from expected better halves.

• Charming/careless: These include humor; however, they can likewise be messy or even cowardly. These are the average "pickup line," like "Did it hurt when you tumbled from paradise?" or "You realize what might look perfect on you? Me." as a general rule, all kinds of people rank these as the most un-favored choice to get from a possible significant other.

• Your relationship system will likewise assume a part in picking an opener. Studies propose that individuals going for something long haul will almost certain utilization a legit and steady ploy, while individuals going for something transient will more probably use control or untrustworthiness. In the event that it's affection you're searching for, go for genuine and steady like clockwork.

1.Convince her to see you. Accomplish something that will make her consider you. However, try not to attempt to make yourself into something you're not. Acting naturally (perhaps the most ideal variant of you) is the most effective way to guarantee that assuming she's keen on you, she's truly inspired by you, not someone you're attempting to be to get yourself taken note.

• Deal with yourself. Practice good eating habits, exercise, and dress in garments that express something about you. You don't need to be a style model or a hotshot competitor, yet keeping yourself slick, clean, and prepped will flaunt your actual wellbeing, which people have developed to see as naturally appealing.

• Concentrates on show that lady's esteem social qualities, like empathy and agreeableness, as exceptionally (or considerably more) than actual appeal. Accomplish something that shows you care about others. Volunteer at your nearby food bank, give blood, rescue a companion of a dilemma, put together a foundation closeout. Show her that there's something else to you besides what might be expected. She'll be intrigued that you offer in return and inquisitive about what else you bring to the table.

• Show her your entertaining side. Research shows that all kinds of people rank a funny bone as perhaps of the most alluring quality in an expected accomplice. Mess around, make others snicker - - simply don't disparage or utilize mean or harsh humor, since that is a dependable method for killing the state of mind immediately. A little fun-loving nature is likewise liable to help you.

• Succeed at something you're great at, ideally in her organization. What do you get along admirably? It very well may be anything from tennis, rock climbing, or football, to go along with, math, or discussion.

While you're dating somebody, you frequently think of yourself as contemplating whether your person doesn't joke around about you. A few men are simply not all that great at communicating their feelings, which makes it hard to know his sentiments. Furthermore, you might coincidentally find folks who show they truly care however as a general rule, they don't care a lot about you. And afterward there are folks who are guardians - one that concedes their affection and treats you with adoration. So how might you let know if the person you're with really and profoundly cherishes you?

He probably won't communicate his adoration verbally; however, he could give indications that he is blindly enamored with you. It is high contrast assuming you ask us. At the point when someone really cherishes you, you simply know since they cause you to feel exceptional in a manner nobody has at any point finished. Yet, on the off chance that you're actually contemplating whether he's enamored with you or not, read on to know the obvious signs he is frantically infatuated with you.

Part 2

120 signs he cherishes

The following are 120 signs he cherishes you profoundly.

He sets aside a few minutes for you

Everybody is occupied and they can drop designs constantly. In any case, not with your man. He carves out opportunity to accompany you and see you, regardless of whether it's for a brief period.

He encourages you

Men like to cause a lady to have a good sense of security and safeguarded when they're infatuated with her. They don't be guaranteed to have to take someone's teeth on a mission to cause you to trust that. He will simply be there close by in troublesome times.

He regards your perspective

He regards your choice in any event, when you all have various sentiments. He considers all that you say, in any event, when he disagrees with you.

He stays faithful to his commitments

He is a dependably trustworthy man. A man who regards and loves you will constantly stay faithful to his obligations. Indeed, he could neglect a few little subtleties yet not the large ones that matter in the relationship.

He acquaints you with his loved ones

Individuals who don't mess around with somebody, they don't conceal it from their loved ones. They possibly keep their relationship when they feel that the situation work figures out soon. In this way, on the off chance that your person acquaints you with his loved ones - he is most certainly enamored with you.

He needs more closeness

We are not discussing sexual closeness here; we're discussing the irregular jabs or never passing up on an opportunity to embrace you. In the event that he cherishes you, he will feel a consistent need to hold your hand, kiss or essentially care for you.

He doesn't pass judgment on you for your absurdity

Here and there ladies truly do act a piece insane, some more than others. Yet, your man wouldn't fret the insane in you and you don't feel timid to act naturally when you're with them. They cause you to feel great in your skin without making a decision about you for anything.

He upholds your fantasies

The principal sign of genuine affection is that your accomplice upholds you to follow the way you've picked, instead of attempting to make one for you. Any other way, it very well may be hard picking between the individual you love and what you're intended to do.

He starts contact

On the off chance that you notice an expansion in the quantity of texts or calls, that is perfect! This implies he needs to hear your voice and appreciates having discussions with you.

Compromise is a two-way road in your relationship

Several needs to make specific tradeoffs in a relationship. However, in some cases one accomplice closes us forfeiting more than the other one. Nonetheless, when you see the tradeoffs are not coming just from your side, then that is a colossal sign your man loves you.

Review how much fun it was to love your soul mate like crazy, quite a long time ago when everything was new and particularly captivating? That is the clarification you proposed. That is the explanation you got hitched. That is what you had as an essential worry for the rest of your life.

Then, when in doubt, life disturbs the general stream and everything - and that consolidates associations at home - is in danger of sneaking past into unexceptional. Exhaustion prompts more exhaustion and subsequently, in the blink of an eye, we have the viewpoint that acknowledges, "This is all that is important" and we should be prepared to settle since, "In light of everything, everyone does, don't they?"

Taking everything into account; no. Mind-desensitizing comparability isn't exactly the fundamental decision. You can see the value in marriage with excitement and verve. Endeavor the going with 10 techniques for appreciating your significant other like crazy:

1. Pick Love: We have such a ton of effect over how we feel. Get up in the initial segment of the day with the choice to revere your soul mate like crazy forthcoming. While you're having that perspective, you'll most likely pour her some coffee or serve her tea. By and by you have a positive impact going and it's everything since you made a mindful choice.

2. Reliably for seven days: Make an obligation - to yourself - to achieve something to some degree faltering reliably for seven days. Then, at that point, own beginning and end to the end. It might be basically essentially as fundamental as a lone rose at home… or it might be essentially pretty much as shocking as surprising her with a reverence tune (by you) in a public spot. Regardless, by the third day, you'll be amped available too.

3. Propose to her again: Get on one knee (if you really can!) and tell her all over about how you'd a lot of need to utilize whatever is left of your life as her soul mate. Consider all of the reasons you love her then; show her the sum you do.

4. Trust it: There's a standard that articulates, "If you trust something to be substantial, it is!" Let yourself know you love her like crazy - trust it. How about we expect it without keeping down. Put everything in order. It will be substantial.

5. Examine her: And guarantee it's certain. Keep your soul mate to you, on your heart, and in a positive light. Research proposes it takes seven up-sides of equilibrium one negative. Without a doubt, load those opportunities to ceaselessly talk your significant other up. To your buddies, at work, at church, to various relatives… it has no effect where you are or who you're speaking with, talk about your soul mate and you will treasure her more.

6. Hold her: You've had some significant awareness of the five principal roads for warmth, right? For sure,

women convey in more than one language and one of them is for the most part "hold me." A significant, long hug when you get back. Catching hands walking and in the vehicle. Snuggling on the couch. You name what is happening - by and by add some variation of "hold me". It's shared advantage, and it will help you with treasuring her like crazy.

7. Hang out: Sound like a simple choice? For sure, it is! Nevertheless, halting our brains is a commonplace eccentricity for men, so this one comes to the overview. Be together and recall that it is so wonderful to simply hang out. Shared trait can raise love, not just contempt.

8. Make it unprecedented: It's exorbitantly easy to save special for other people, and thereafter confine ourselves

- and our fundamental relationship - to OK, but definitely not great.

9. Convey her picture in your wallet: Don't just truck the picture around, yet show her off too. "Hi, check out at this inconceivable pic of my soul mate!" "Your grandkids look delightful… but look at this new photo of my life partner."

10. Tell her "Thankful" reliably:

Here are the most heartfelt thank you for cherishing me this much statements and saying for a darling that will turn into the best ever for you, assuming that you send it to your better half, spouse, sweetheart or sweetheart in appreciation for the love the person in question shows towards you. You have been there like a mother, a dad, a sibling, and everything. Gratitude for cherishing me bounty. Good health.

2. In some cases, I consider the times I had worked alone and I can't however see the value in your presence in my life. You've shown me what genuine fellowship is. Gratitude for cherishing me this much.

Words smell the tables of letters to portray you. You are an epitome of beauty and love. Much thanks to you for cherishing me for me.

4. What is existence without solace? What is torment without a salve? The outcome is passing. From the depts of depts, thank you for continuously being there. Much obliged to you for adoring me.

In the event that desires were blossoms, I would get you a lot of them to show exactly the amount I love and value your quintessence. Much obliged to you for cherishing me like no other.

6. Here and there, you just get persuaded to continue to battle since you have a few people you would rather not dishearten. You are one of them, Dear. Your adoration and faith in me have presented to me this far. Gratitude for cherishing me. Life is just of stages. You pass each for certain little challenges; hardships simplified as a result of impact. Gratitude for cherishing me more honey.

My dream comes from you fog of the times. Presently I need to have of you. Be that as it may, before then, at that point, gratitude for cherishing me much, dear.

9. Our organization is a cosmetic of companions, family and fans. Family criticisms you. Companions rouse and remain by you. Fans cheer you. You, my dear, are a

family and companion. Gratitude for cherishing me enough.

My life counts multiple times as a result of you. Gratitude for ceaseless love and faith in me. You remain ever dear. Good health.

You hold a spot in my heart, you are everything I'll at any point require. Much thanks to you for being that one cherishing me like Jesus.

You are unique to me my solitary genuine companion. Everlastingly, show up for one another. Gratitude for cherishing me as I do.

The downpour has beaten me; the sun also has grinned. You were there in downpour and sun. Gratitude for being my defensive layer. Gratitude for adoring me.

14. You give pleasure and satisfaction to my spirit each time I'm around you. I love you, and gratitude for adoring me back.

You are more valuable than gold and silver. Place 3,000,000 naira and you for myself and run with you. Gratitude for cherishing me, dear.

My mom advised me to take off from ladies; run and never think back she would agree. In any case, I figure I ought to run with you consistently. Gratitude for being there. Gratitude for adoring me like one.

17. Working with you has shown me 1,000,000 things I can never learn all alone. Gratitude for being my instructor and tutor.

www.ingramcontent.com/pod-product-compliance
Lightning Source LLC
LaVergne TN
LVHW020537160826
845677LV00015B/4103

9798847009867